GIRL

Pony Club

Jacqueline Arena

illustrated by
Lloyd Foye

MACMILLAN

First published in 2008 by
MACMILLAN EDUCATION AUSTRALIA PTY LTD
15–19 Claremont Street, South Yarra 3141

Visit our website at www.macmillan.com.au or
go directly to www.macmillanlibrary.com.au

Associated companies and representatives throughout the world.

National Library of Australia
Cataloguing-in-Publication data

Arena, Jacqueline.
Pony club.

   For primary school students.
   ISBN 978 1 4202 6147 9 (pbk.).
   ISBN 978 1420262179 (set 3)

   1. Horsemanship – Juvenile fiction. 2. Show jumping –
   Juvenile fiction. I. Title. (Series: Girlz rock!).

A 823.4

Series created by Felice Arena and Phil Kettle
Project management by Limelight Publishing Services Pty Ltd
Cover and text design by Lore Foye
Illustrations by Lloyd Foye

Printed in China

GiRLZ ROCK!

Contents

Rachel   Ellie

CHAPTER 1

Big Black Stallion

Best friends Ellie and Rachel are about to have their first private horse-riding lesson. They patiently wait for their instructor to appear.

Rachel "I'm so excited. This is going to be so cool. I hope I get to ride that one over there."

Ellie "Which one?"

Rachel "That one."

Dressed in full riding gear, the girls wander over to a yard with stables and horses. They climb up on to the wooden fence to take a closer look.

Ellie "You mean that big black stallion?"

Rachel "Yeah. Isn't he beautiful? Look at him prancing around. He's a star."

Ellie "Um, Rach, Mum said that the gift vouchers she got for us, for this first lesson, are for beginners only. Beginners don't ride stallions. We'll probably ride those ponies over there. That's why it's a pony club, get it?"

Rachel "Ponies? Ponies are for babies. And besides, they're dumb! I want to ride a real horse—really fast."

Ellie "Ponies are not dumb! They may be smaller than horses, but that doesn't make them dumb. They're just as intelligent and beautiful as horses are. I was reading somewhere that ponies are …"

Ellie continues to chat about all the information she has read about horses and ponies and doesn't notice that Rachel has climbed over the fence into the horse yard.

Ellie "So, if you look at all the facts, you'll see that ponies are actually very smart. Don't you think? Rach?"

Ellie suddenly notices that Rachel is making her way over towards the stallion.

Ellie (shouting) "Rachel! What are you doing? You're not meant to be in there. He might hurt you. Stop! Don't!"

CHAPTER 2

He's Behind You

Rachel slowly inches closer to the stallion.

Ellie "Rachel, don't! You don't know what his temperament is like."

Rachel "His what?"

Ellie "His mood—if he's a happy horse or an angry horse."

Rachel "Oh, well he looks pretty happy to me, don't you, boy? Don't be scared. I'm just coming over to say hello."

Suddenly the stallion snorts and shakes his head from side to side. Rachel squeals.

Ellie "See. I don't think it's safe. Please come back, Rach."

Rachel "Hmmm, yeah, I think you're right, El."

Ellie "Just turn around slowly so you won't startle him."

Rachel turns away from the stallion and softly steps back towards Ellie, talking the whole time.

Rachel "Hey, El, I wonder what's taking that instructor and your mum so long. How many forms do they have to fill out before we take our lesson?"

Ellie doesn't answer Rachel.

Rachel "Ellie? I said how many forms do you think ... El, what's wrong?"

Ellie "Don't look now, Rach, but he's coming."

Rachel "Who's coming?"

Ellie "The stallion. He's following you. In fact, he's right behind you."

Rachel "He's what?"

Rachel freezes, staring straight at
Ellie. The stallion is now standing
directly behind her. Rachel can feel
him breathing down her neck.

Rachel (frightened) "Ellie, help me.
What am I going to do?"

CHAPTER THREE

A Fairytale Horse

The stallion begins to nibble at Rachel's helmet.

Rachel "Oh, no, he's going to eat me."

Ellie "Don't move, Rach. Horses can smell fear."

Rachel "Well, I'm in trouble then, 'cause I'm really scared, El. Ahhh! What's he doing now?"

The stallion playfully nudges Rachel forward.

Rachel "El, he's pushing me. He's gonna kill me!"

Ellie begins to giggle.

Rachel "What's so funny? Any
second now this stallion is gonna
jump up onto his back legs and ..."
Ellie "And do a dance for you?"
Rachel "No! He's gonna ..."
Ellie "Do a handstand!"

Rachel "NO! Crush me with his
hooves! El, how can you joke at a
time like this?"

Ellie "Because he's not a killer.
It looks like he has a nice
temperament. He's a happy horse."

Rachel "He is?"

Ellie climbs over the fence and into the yard to join Rachel. She gently pats the stallion. Rachel turns and does the same thing.

Rachel "See. I told you he's a big softie."

Ellie "Yeah, right."

Rachel "Now I really want to ride him."

Ellie "Me too."

Rachel "He's like one of those
horses in those fairytale books. The
perfect horse for a princess. Yeah,
a princess, that's me. Princess
Rachel on her trusty stallion, Bob."

Ellie "Bob? Don't you mean, Sir
Bob? It sounds more important
that way. And if you're Princess
Rachel, who am I?"

Rachel "You're my maid and best friend, Maid El. Together we ride Sir Bob in search of a prince for me and a ... um ... a milkshake blender for you."

Ellie "I don't like the sound of this. Then what?"

Rachel "I don't know. You're the one who reads heaps of books. You tell the story."

Ellie "Okay, I will ..."

CHAPTER 4

A Galloping Adventure

The girls continue to gently pat the stallion, as Ellie thinks for a moment.

Ellie "Okay, um ... I've got it! We ride Sir Bob deep into a forest. Until we discover ..."

Rachel "A McDonald's?"

Ellie "No. We discover a …"

Rachel "A giant walking and talking doll that looks like me?"

Ellie "No, there's no doll and no McDonald's. We discover a hidden city."

Rachel "Oh."

Ellie "And we ride into the city square. But there's no-one around. The streets are empty."

Rachel "Why? Is everyone inside?"

Ellie "Maybe."

Rachel "I bet they're watching my all-time favourite TV show, *Home and School*. Last night Brad said he liked Bethany but Bethany really likes Dylan and …"

Ellie "Rach! I'm telling the story here."

Rachel "Sorry."

Ellie "Anyway, there's no-one around but suddenly, hundreds of elves on ponies come out of hiding and ambush us."

Rachel "Why?"

Ellie "Well, the king elf comes forward and says that we are his prisoners because we, or really you, said that ponies are dumb. And since their city is called Pony Club City, the capital of Pony Club Kingdom, well, they're not happy with us."

Rachel "But I didn't mean to say it."

Ellie "Well, they don't know that. And as they come to tie us up, we suddenly ..."

Rachel "Scream?"

Ellie "No."

Rachel "Call my mum on my mobile phone?"

Ellie "No. We make a run for it. Well, we get Sir Bob to make a run for it."

Rachel "Giddy-up, Sir Bob!"

Ellie "Yeah, and the chase is on."

CHAPTER 5

Our Prince

Ellie continues the story.

Ellie "We ride Sir Bob past the king elf and through the streets of Pony Club City."

Rachel "And we jump over chicken cages and tables, just like they do in the movies."

Ellie "But the elves on their ponies are right behind us. Sir Bob has to gallop faster or they'll catch us."

Rachel ruffles the stallion's mane.

Rachel "I bet you can gallop super-fast, can't you boy?"

Ellie "We finally make it out of the hidden city. But just as we're almost through the forest, a wild pig runs out of a bush and spooks Sir Bob—and we're thrown off."

Rachel "Oh no! What happens next? And what about Sir Bob?"

Ellie "Sir Bob runs off into the forest and leaves us behind."

Rachel "No!"

Ellie "Yes. And we can hear the elves getting closer."

Rachel "Oh, no, we're gonna get caught."

Ellie "But suddenly, a prince on a white stallion appears from out of the forest. And he has Sir Bob with him, on a lead. He gallantly brings Sir Bob back to us."

Rachel "So we jump back on Sir Bob."

Ellie "Yes, just before the elves get there. And the prince leads us back here, to the riding school. He saves us. And that's the end."

Rachel "I love that story, El! But what about your milkshake blender?"

Ellie shakes her head. Her mother and the riding instructor arrive. The instructor says she's pleased they've met Prince, the riding school stallion.

Ellie "Prince? Sir Bob is Prince?"

The girls squeal. The instructor asks if the girls are ready for their first riding lesson.

Ellie "Yes. Just so long as we don't have to ride anywhere near Pony Club Kingdom."

Rachel "And just so long as we get to ride on ponies and not horses. Sorry, Sir Bob, I mean Prince, but maybe it's safer that way for all of us! We want to be sure the hidden city stays hidden for a while longer."

Rachel

GIRLZ ROCK!
Pony Lingo

Ellie

giddy-up! This is what you say when you want your horse to move—especially if you're being chased by evil elves.

horse poop Something you don't want to step in or land on top of. Ewwww!!!

horse-riding instructors They are the best people to teach you how to ride a horse.

prance When horses dance or spring forward on their hind legs. Maybe someone should create a TV pony show called *Prancing with the Stars!*

temperament A fancy word for "mood". It's used to describe horses or dogs. What's your temperament?

GIRLZ ROCK!
Pony Must-dos

☆ Never approach a horse or a pony if you're not sure of its temperament. He or she could be in a really bad mood.

☆ When you're riding, wear a tight-fitting shirt or jumper—tucked in. It may not be a good look, but big, flowing, loose shirts can get caught on the saddle or other equipment.

☆ Always listen to your horse-riding instructor. They know everything about horses—and will help make you the best horse rider in the universe! Well, at least in your pony club.

☆ If you want to learn how to ride, leave brochures and magazines around the house so your parents will get the hint.

☆ Wear a helmet—it comes in handy if a stallion wants to nibble at your head.

☆ Before you go riding try getting into a horse mood. Watch the movies *Spirit, Stallion of the Cimmaron* or *Black Beauty.*

☆ Never walk around the back of a horse unless your riding instructor says it's safe to, or if you were actually planning to be kicked to the Moon!

☆ Take photos of you and your pony so you can print them out and stick them all over your bedroom walls. Remember to ask the pony for permission to take its photo—it's always polite!

GIRLZ ROCK!
Pony Instant Info

☙ There are pony club organisations in over 30 countries in the world.

☙ Ponies are usually shorter than horses. They also have a thicker mane, a shorter head and a wider body.

☙ A stallion is a male horse and a mare is a female horse. A foal is a baby horse.

☙ Any marking on a horse's forehead is called a star—even if it isn't shaped like one.

☙ The biological classification name for a horse is *Equus caballus*.

☙ Some vets can sometimes tell the age of a pony by looking at its teeth.

A person who makes shoes for horses and who clips their hooves is called a farrier.

The oldest recorded horse was an English barge horse called Old Billy. Old Billy lived to be 62 years old. The average life span of a horse is 20 to 25 years.

A group of ponies or horses is called a herd.

GIRLZ ROCK!
Think Tank

1 A pony is generally bigger than a horse. True or False?

2 What does a horse-riding instructor do?

3 What's the most important thing you should wear when you go horse riding?

4 Sir Bob (or Prince) is a mare. True or False?

5 What's another way of describing a horse's mood? It starts with "T".

6 Where would you find Pony Club Kingdom?

7 What's the horse's mane?

8 What does "giddy-up!" mean?

Answers

1 False. Ponies are generally smaller than horses.

2 A horse-riding instructor is a person who's going to teach you how to ride a horse or pony.

3 The most important thing you should wear is a helmet.

4 False. Sir Bob (or Prince) is a proud stallion!

5 Another word for a horse's mood is temperament.

6 Pony Club Kingdom is deep, deep in the forest.

7 A horse's mane is the long hair that runs along the horse's neck.

8 "Giddy-up!" means "Hurry up, horse. Let's get outta here!"

How did you score?

- If you got all 8 answers correct, then get out your riding boots. You're pony mad! You can't get enough of ponies! What are you waiting for? Ask your parents if they can book you in for your first riding lesson!

- If you got 6 answers correct, then you like ponies and would love to read a good pony story or watch a good horse movie. You probably had a soft toy pony when you were a baby.

- If you got fewer than 4 answers correct, you'd rather ride your bike!

Hey girls!

I hope that you have as much fun reading my story as I have had writing it. I loved reading and writing stories when I was growing up ... I still do!

Here are some suggestions that might help you enjoy reading even more than you do now. At school, why don't you use "Pony Club" as a play? And you and your friends can be the actors. Get a horse-riding helmet (a bike helmet will do), some high boots (gumboots will do) and a broom (to be your pony or horse) to use as props.

So ... have you decided who is going to be Rachel and who is going to be Ellie? And what about the narrator?

Now act out the story in front of your friends ... you'll have a great time! You also might like to take this story home and get someone in your family to read it with you. Maybe they can take on a part in the story.

Whatever you choose to do, remember, reading and writing is a whole lot of fun ... and girls totally rock!

Take care,

Jacqueline Saena

Jacqueline talked to Holly, another *Girlz Rock!* author.

Jacqueline "When I was younger I always dreamt of having my very own pony."

Holly "Me too!"

Jacqueline "But we didn't have the room for it."

Holly "Me too!"

Jacqueline "It would've been happy in my backyard. That's what I said to my mum."

Holly "Me too!"

Jacqueline "Can you stop saying 'me too!'"

Holly "Okay … I love ponies!"

Jacqueline "Me too!"

GIRLZ ROCK!
What a Laugh!

Q Why did the pony cough?

A He was a little hoarse!

GIRLZROCK!

Read about the fun that girls have in these *GIRLZROCK!* titles:

Birthday Party Bedlam

Pony Club

Doubles Trouble

Soccer Crazy

Dance Fever

Minigolf Face-off

Trapeze Dreams

Two at the Zoo

... and 20 more great titles to choose from!